LIVE FULLY COLORING BOOK FOR ENNEAGRAM TYPE 1

The Reformer

D1613389

POSITIVE MESSAGES & AFFIRMATIONS COLORING BOOK TO BE YOUR BEST SELF

(ENNEAGRAM GROWTH SERIES)

THANK YOU FOR YOUR PURCHASE

Table of Contents

Introduction

In this book, you will find a brief review of the nine basic personality structures of the Enneagram, their additional dimensions, or wings, as well as common strengths and unique challenges for each specific personality type and the 5 stages of growth. With this knowledge, you'll be able to start your personal growth and positive transformations to live life fully with 25 beautiful coloring pages of affirmations and messages for your specific Enneagram type .

What Is the Enneagram?

Simply put, the Enneagram is a personality system that describes how different types of people manage their feelings and see the world (Newgent et. al., 2004). This happens in certain patterns, and these patterns make for nine different types of personalities. These personality types can be illustrated by a diagram, which shows how different types of personalities interact with one another.

The term Enneagram originates from the Greek language, combining the words for "nine" (*ennea*) and "writing" (*gramma*). The Enneagram personality types, their dominant traits, and more importantly, advice for how one grows and prospers based on their personality type is what has made the Enneagram one of the more popular personality theories today.

So, what do you get from studying your Enneagram personality type? While you're going to have to take a test to find out which Enneagram type you are, you can use the valuable information about typical core beliefs, fundamental motivations and fears, and typical worldview perspective to better understand yourself and people around you.

But, why do you need this knowledge? Core beliefs make up our mindset, worldview, perspective, and overall how we approach people, events, and situations. While not all core beliefs are flawed, some could be holding you back from reaching your full potential. You see, we form core beliefs during infancy, while we're still unable to accurately understand how the world works—hence the confusion with life and many exaggerations and inaccuracies that follow, difficulties that are common to the human experience.

The 9 Enneagram Personality Type

When your outlook on the world and life is shaped by limiting beliefs, you can get blindsided by wrong assumptions, either positive or negative. Then, if you experience something that opposes your beliefs, confusion follows, often resulting in fear, anxiety, and even depression (Sutton et. al., 2013). So, how do we work around innate misjudgments that are holding us back? Find out your Enneagram type, and learn how to work with it! According to the Enneagram, your personality falls within a range of the following nine types:

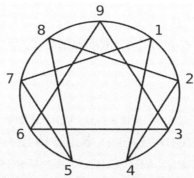

Each type has a sense of how the world is, how they need to be in the world and strategies o survive in the world

Type One: The Reformer a.k.a The Perfectionist/—"I'm a Perfectionist ..."

This personality type is idealistic and rational. They lead by principle and have habits of self-control and perfectionism. Emma Watson, Julie Andrews, and Natalie Portman share this inclination towards hard work, order, and discipline. Balance, goodness, continuous improvement and integrity are the reformer's true gifts, but they can also become resentful and work extremely hard to avoid mistakes and losing control.

Type Two: The Helper a.k.a The Altruist/Giver—"I Must Help People ..."

Generous, kind and sometimes people-pleasing, this type is a caring personality who likes to show their affection. They are also good at understanding the needs of others but often ignore their own needs. Jennifer Garner, Dolly Parton, and Doris Gray represent the type of an altruist who is patient and caring but can become resentful, possessive and codependent. Their innate fear is being unloved, so their egos may fixate on flattery as an overcompensation.

Type Three: High Achiever a.k.a The Performer/Motivator—"I Strive To Be ..."

If you have anything in common with Will Smith, Tom Cruise, and Oprah Winfrey, it is the pragmatic, success-oriented, and driven outlook on life. Threes are driven to achieve big goals to earn praise and validation from others, adopting characteristics of those they perceive as successful to accomplish this. However, Threes can also become obsessed, extremely competitive and exploitative in their pursuit of success. With the core fear of being useless and a failure, they strive to be invaluable and may become vain in that pursuit.

Type Four: The Individualist a.k.a The Romantic/Dreamer—"I'm Fascinated by What's Below the Surface ..."

If you're artistic, sensitive, and withdrawn, you may have something in common with acclaimed artists like Johnny Depp, Kate Winslet, and Judy Garland. Fours can deeply connect with their emotions and sometimes feel something is missing. However, if overemphasized, these personality traits can lead to depression, alienation, and self-destructive behaviors. Fours fear losing their sense of identity and significance and can become melancholic when feeling lost.

Type Five: Investigators a.k.a The Thinker/Observe—"I Need To Know ..."

Greta Garbo, Ralph Fiennes, and Daniel Day-Lewis all share profound curiosity, desire to learn, and fierce independence. But, personalities like these can become lonely and detached from reality when pursuing goals and even become consumed by dark ideas. They fear having their energy depleted, being helpless and incompetent, so striving towards mastery and understanding is a part of overcoming this fear.

Type Six: Loyalist a.k.a The Questioner/ Anxious Anticipators—"I'm Not Good Enough ..."

Loyal, brave, and reliable, Sixes like Tom Hanks, Robert Pattison, and JesseEisenberg are wonderful to work with and super dependable. This yields success but constant worry about their potential for failure and worse case scenarios can make them eccentric and self-destructive. These personalities strive towards having guidance and heavily rely on preparing for the worse. Being without guidance is their basic fear, and as such, they may fixate on worry.

Type Seven: Charismatic Enthusiasts a..k.a The Entertainer —"I Want To Experience ..."

Seven's are optimistic, upbeat, positive and flexible but fear missing out. Dick Van Dyke, Robin Williams, and Elizabeth Taylor are said to be agile, energetic, and adventure-seeking. But, if overemphasized, these traits can cause erratic and impulsive behaviors and even result in self-destructive outcomes. Sevens can become obsessed with planning as a part of their ultimate mission to seek satisfaction and to avoid negative emotions or feeling deprived or trapped.

Type Eight: Intense Challengers a.k.a The Protector—"I want ..."

Powerful and dominant, the challengers are persistent, willful and a great defender of others. But, they can also become confrontational, irresponsible, and arrogant. Kathleen Turner, Frank Sinatra, and Marlon Brando are all said to have these traits. Their core need is to protect themselves and those they care about from harm, and they fear being hurt, sometimes to the point of becoming vengeful. They seek truth, which gives them a sense of purpose.

Type Nine: Zen Peace-Seekers a.k.a The Mediator—"I Enjoy the Beauty of Life ..."

People like Keanu Reeves, Audrey Hepburn, and Morgan Freeman are agreeable, easy-going, and introspective. Nines make good mediators, being open minded, calm and adaptable. On the downside, Nines can become neglectful, disoriented, and detached from their true feelings. Nines tend to avoid conflict and discomfort. In their effort to find wholeness, those who seek peace dread loss and separation. They may resort to too much daydreaming in their endless pursuit of love.

The Three Centers of Intelligence: Head, Heart, and Body

In the Enneagram, the nine personality types are grouped in threes by each center. What does this mean? It means that a certain source of intelligence (body, mind, heart) is dominant in a particular set of three personality types. However, this doesn't mean that a personality type has a single intelligence center. Instead, the center in which a personality type resides is often distorted, or detached from it by the person's ego.

Self-awareness is the best way to understand where our strengths lie, so that we can access our natural strength and vitality sources. This is achieved with integration, a process during which you heighten the awareness of all three sources of intelligence, often done best with mindfulness and meditation.

The Instinctive Center—Body- The body is a source of survival, vitality, and all life. This center houses types one, eight, and nine

The Feeling Center—Heart- This center houses personality types two, three, and four

The Thinking Center—Head- This center houses personalities five, six, and seven

What Are Wings?

Not a single person is a pure type of an Enneagram personality. Everyone is unique and has certain traits that "belong" to other personality types as well. Aside from the basic personality type, people also have a mixture of that type, plus one or two personality types from the Enneagram's chart. These adjacent personality types are called "wings."

While the basic Enneagram type dominates your personality, the wings complement these traits and add colorful elements to your character. It is also possible to possess strong traits of "neighboring" types. For example, if your personality type is three, your "wings" might include traits and characteristics of Twos and Fours.

Some Enneagram schools claim that a person can have both wings, while others acknowledge only one. However, it is important to note that all traits found in the Enneagram exist in each person to some degree. What makes a difference is a particular set of strong and weak sides, the first contributing to growth and maturation, and the latter holding you back from living a fulfilled life.

Growth and maturation also play a role in how your personality changes over time, which may affect your wing-traits as well. Aging brings valuable insight and wisdom, and people can grow in a certain direction, depending on their experiences, circumstances, and natural inclinations.

How To Find Out Your Type (Dominant Pattern)

Despite the ease of taking a test, discovering your dominant type can be tricky with the Enneagram. Although viewing it as a set of nine distinct types of personalities seems like the easiest way to go, it isn't always the most accurate.

Once you finish your Enneagram test, one of the types will stand out as your basic personality type. Your basic personality type is formed in early childhood.

This is when your inborn temperament and genetic factors interact with your experiences to form a particular set of traits, which makes for your dominant Enneagram type. This dominant personality type determines how you'll adapt to your immediate environment. It also shapes how you unconsciously view parental figures.

Children as young as five begin to understand that they are separate entities from their environment and the people in it, and they begin to build a sense of self. However, the emulsion of intertwined genetic, environmental, and temperamental factors has already formed a steady, dominant personality structure that will stay with them for the rest of their life.

The best way to identify your basic personality type is to take the Riso-Hudson Enneagram Type Indicator test, which will identify your dominant personality type. The result of this test will provide basic understanding of the basic personality traits that describe you. Many other tests can be found on the internet, just search "Enneagram Test"

Growth & Transformation

As you learned in earlier paragraphs, each Enneagram type comes with distinct strengths and struggles. Like anything if your strengths are overused or the core personality patterns are relied on too heavily, the type can run the show, causing you to get in your own way and not get the best from life.

Luckily for you, there are numerous strategies that you can use to grow as a person. When used regularly and diligently, these strategies will assure that you've matured and that you no longer suffer the distortions that come with your inborn temperament. The Enneagram patterns are structured by what we call a Universal Growth Process, or UGP. This process consists of the following stages:

The Stage of Awareness

Becoming able to observe how certain personality traits guide your thinking, decisions, actions, and of course, their consequences, is useful, as it can help you establish better self-control. At the beginning of your growth journey, you won't be able to quickly change whichever temperament quirks make your life difficult. Instead, you will be able to observe and control your actions, disabling them from making your life difficult. Taking a moment to stop and breathe helps increase awareness.

The Stage of Acceptance

Learning how to open up to kindness and acceptance of yourself and others, particularly when you're upset and angry, helps you relieve inner tension and anxiety. Kindness begins to replace self-criticism, and over time you begin to find yourself thinking in completely different directions. This, of course, creates different, better experiences and consequences. Positive affirmations and messages can aid kindness.

The Stage of Appreciation

During this stage, you will start to realize that you are neglecting the positives at the expense of highlighting negatives. You may become more willing to think about people's pleasant traits instead of being irritated by their flaws, and you may be more willing to absorb positive circumstances of a situation over the negative ones. Appreciation makes you more compassionate, first with yourself, reducing inner self-criticism and negative self-talk, and then with others, making you more agile, assertive, and agreeable.

The Stage of Action

The stage of making changes to the way you react on emotional, cognitive, and temperamental levels starts when your core beliefs begin to shift. Instead of acting on them straightaway, you become able to notice, take a step back, recollect, and contain any unfavorable reaction. You then become able to contemplate your reaction and use a constructive approach to mentor yourself toward more mature patterns.

The Stage of Adherence

Once you become able to first control your actions, and then reactions, experiences, and even views, it means that your core beliefs are changing. The ultimate growth stage is when you remain committed to daily changes. You begin to observe how different situations test or trigger certain core beliefs, and you spot patterns that are not useful. The more you're accepting, non-judgmental, and forgiving during this stage, the better your progress advances.

What Are Affirmations?

Affirmations help you enforce positive aspects of your personality and help you let go of negative patterns. The term itself includes suggestive statements that appeal to certain core beliefs, helping you return to balance and relieve tension, anxiety, fear, and insecurities. One important note about affirmations is that they are only effective when spoken in present tense. This is because your mind lives in the present, and using past and future-tense statements won't resonate with it as believable.

Affirmations are chosen to gently appeal to your core beliefs but also address those that you want to change. For this reason, there are 25 coloring pages with Enneagram-specific affirmations and positive messages for your Enneagram type to support personal growth and enable access all centres of intelligence . Taking the time to color allow you to ponder on the affirmations. It is also important to remember that affirmations must feel believable to you in order to be effective. To help your mind be receptive to the messages you may want to begin the affirmation with "MAY I" or "I AM LEARNING TO"

But, how do you say affirmations correctly? It would be the best to practice affirmations daily, out loud with kindness and compassion to yourself. Better yet, stand in front of a mirror, look at your own face as you state encouraging things, as this will make positive affirmations more believable. Now, let's find the right affirmations for your personality type, shall we?

How To Best Use Enneagram Affirmations

Working with the Enneagram can help you better understand yourself and in conjunction with affirmations you can find freedom from inner conflicts, increase your peace within, improve compassion for yourself and others and discover new opportunities by opening access to all centres of intelligence, the heart, head and body allowing you to live a more full life.

You may recognize the traits of your dominant type but remember you are **not** just a type and you can open yourself up to more helpful ways of being. Each morning, stand in front of your mirror and begin stating the affirmations that are best suited to you

It's time to start growing with Enneagram affirmations! The first coloring page describes a superpower of the type. Have fun coloring!

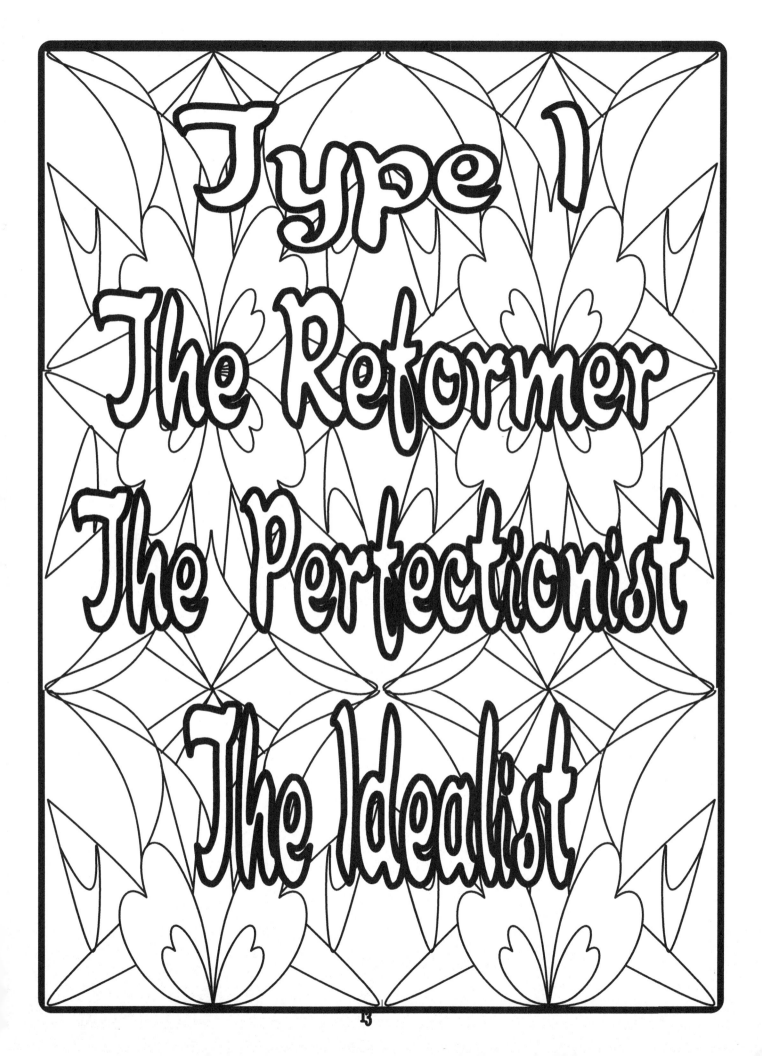

Type 1
The Reformer
The Perfectionist
The Idealist

I bring fairness & principles to the world

I choose to be kind to myself today

I CHOOSE TO VIEW MYSELF WITH KIND EYES

I AM
PERFECTLY
IMPERFECT

26

I AM
FORGIVING OF MYSELF
&
OTHERS

Done is better than perfect

I AM MAKING THE BEST DECISIONS I CAN

It is okay to ask for what I need & want

MAY I
BE MORE
LOVING
THAN
RIGHT

I choose to
be gentle & patient
with myself
& others

I SURRENDER THE NEED TO BE RIGHT

ASKING FOR HELP SHOWS STRENGTH

I welcome other people's ways of doing & being

I embrace there is more than one right way

I accept who I am

I choose to focus on what is right in the world

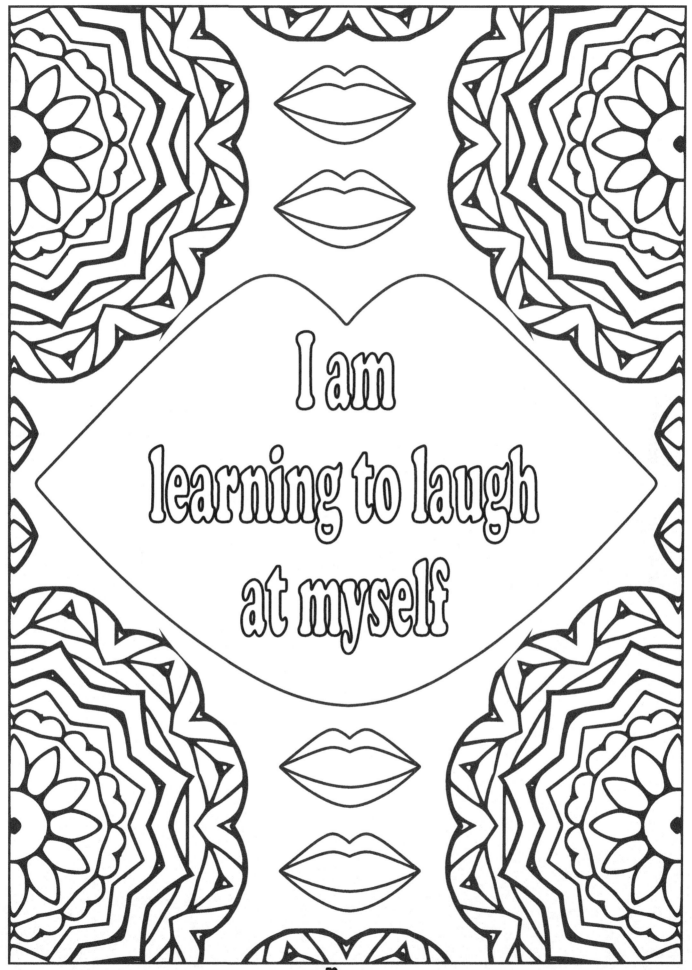

I am
learning to laugh
at myself

May I treat myself with compassion

I love myself just as I am

I RELEASE THE SHOULD DO'S AND EMBRACE WHAT I WANT TO DO

I welcome more fun in my life

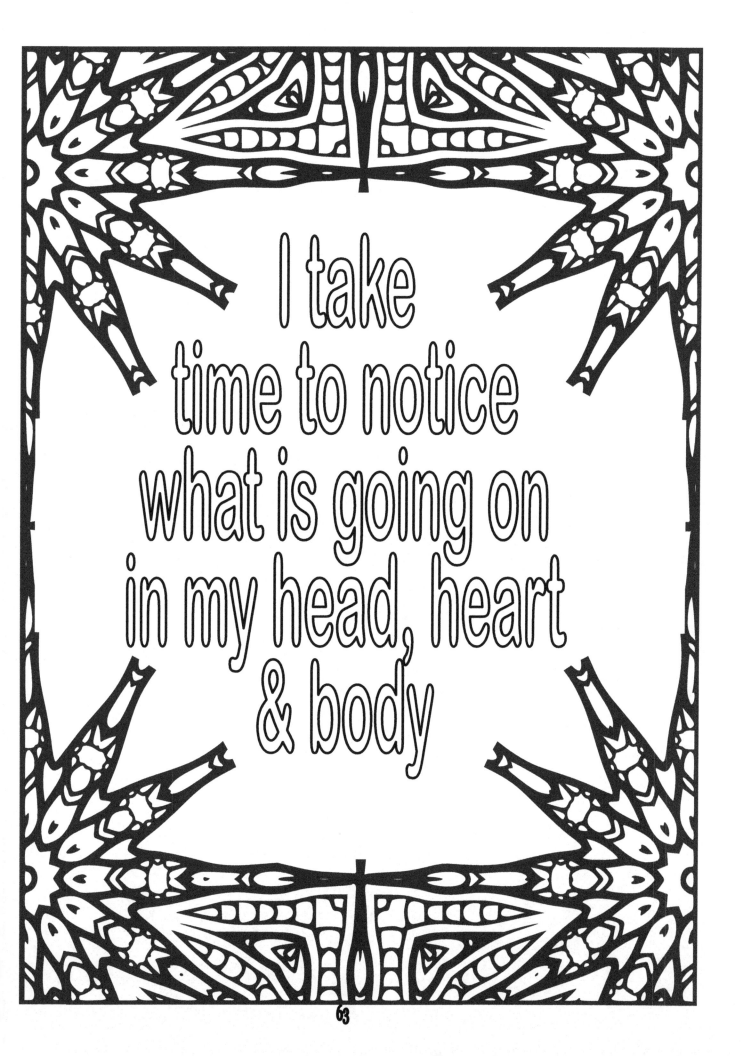

I take
time to notice
what is going on
in my head, heart
& body

Conclusion

Great job! You are ready to start growing and changing. Remember, no one is fully aligned with a single Enneagram personality type. Pay attention to your wings, and take the time to ponder upon how certain personality strengths and weaknesses have affected your life so far. Don't forget to embark on a journey of growth and change, by first becoming aware of negative patterns, and then beginning to accept yourself and other people as they are, so that you're able to notice and change behaviors and beliefs. Good luck!

Check out affirmations for your wings in the following titles:

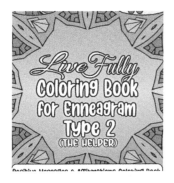 **Live Fully Coloring Book For Enneagram Type 2 (The Helper).**

 **Live Fully Coloring Book For Enneagram Type 9 (Zen Peacekeepers)**

References

Newgent, R. A., Parr, P. H., Newman, I., & Wiggins, K. K. (2004). The Riso-Hudson Enneagram type indicator: Estimates of reliability and validity. *Measurement and evaluation in Counseling and Development*, 36(4), 226-237.

Sutton, A., Allinson, C., & Williams, H. (2013). Personality type and work-related outcomes: An exploratory application of the Enneagram model. *European Management Journal*, 31(3), 234-249.

Made in the USA
Coppell, TX
08 June 2021